CAMBRIDGE INTRODUCTION TO THE HISTORY OF MANKIND · TOPIC BOOK
GENERAL EDITOR · TREVOR CAIRNS

Boudicca's Revolt

Ian Andrews

CAMBRIDGE UNIVERSITY PRESS
Cambridge
London   New York   New Rochelle
Melbourne   Sydney

**Drawings by Graham Humphreys
and Trevor Stubley**

Published by the Press Syndicate of the University of Cambridge
The Pitt Building, Trumpington Street, Cambridge CB2 1RP
32 East 57th Street, New York, NY 10022, USA
296 Beaconsfield Parade, Middle Park, Melbourne 3206,
Australia

Library of Congress Catalogue Card Number 75–189599

© Cambridge University Press 1972

ISBN 0 521 08031 2

First published 1972
Reprinted 1978, 1980

First printed in Great Britain by Jarrold and Sons Ltd, Norwich
Reprinted and bound in Great Britain by
Fakenham Press Limited, Fakenham, Norfolk

Illustrations in this volume are reproduced by kind permission
of the following:
front cover, Gloucester City Museums; back cover,
Verulamium Museum, St Albans; Trustees of the British
Museum, pp.5, 7 (ploughman and Atrebates coin), 12, 32
(shield and helmet), 38, 39, 46, 47 (Towcester head);
University Museum of Archaeology and Ethnology,
Cambridge, pp.3, 7, 42, 44; City of Norwich Museums,
p.7 (Iceni coin); J.K. St Joseph, Cambridge University
Collection, pp.9, 10, 23, 28; Coventry City Museums, p.15;
Colchester and Essex Museum, pp.16, 21, 43 (Castor vase
and Samian mould); Sussex Archaeological Trust, p.18;
National Museum of Wales, p.32 (chariot); Soprintendenza
alle Antichità di Roma p.34; The Mansell Collection, p.35;
The Grosvenor Museum, Chester, p.37; Trustees of the
London Museum, p.41; Verulamium Museum, St Albans,
p.43 (Samian ware); The Warburg Institute, London, p.45;
Gloucester City Museums, p.47 (limestone head of a man);
Bath Spa Committee, p.47 (Gorgon's head).

The author and publisher would like to thank Miss J. Liversidge
and the staff of the Cambridge University Museum of Archaeology and Ethnology for help in collecting illustrations for this
book, though the author accepts responsibility for any errors.

Front cover: A Roman auxiliary cavalryman slays a Briton.
From the first century AD tombstone of Rufus Sita found at
Gloucester.

opposite: British horse trapping made of brass and red
enamel (width $2\frac{3}{4}$ in, 7 cm).

Contents

Pre-Roman migrations to Britain

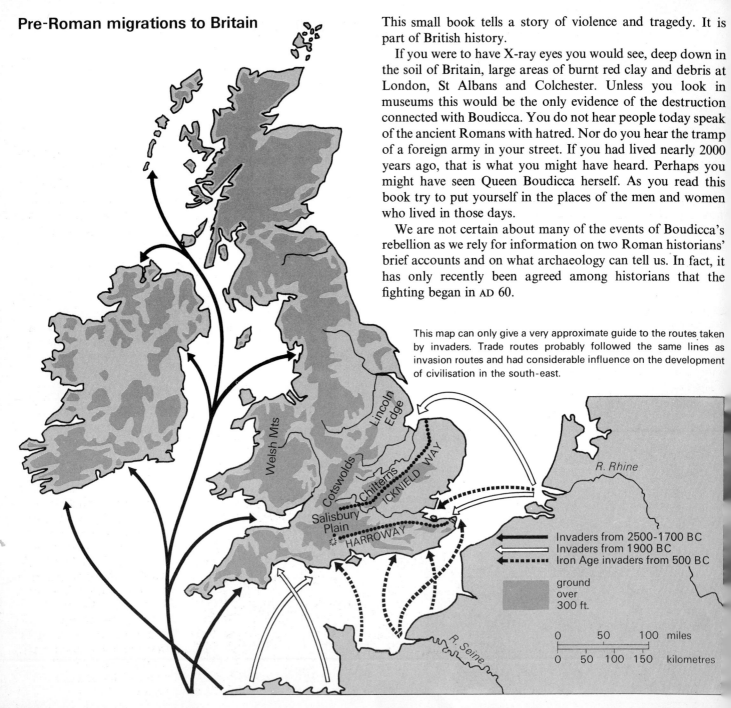

This small book tells a story of violence and tragedy. It is part of British history.

If you were to have X-ray eyes you would see, deep down in the soil of Britain, large areas of burnt red clay and debris at London, St Albans and Colchester. Unless you look in museums this would be the only evidence of the destruction connected with Boudicca. You do not hear people today speak of the ancient Romans with hatred. Nor do you hear the tramp of a foreign army in your street. If you had lived nearly 2000 years ago, that is what you might have heard. Perhaps you might have seen Queen Boudicca herself. As you read this book try to put yourself in the places of the men and women who lived in those days.

We are not certain about many of the events of Boudicca's rebellion as we rely for information on two Roman historians' brief accounts and on what archaeology can tell us. In fact, it has only recently been agreed among historians that the fighting began in AD 60.

This map can only give a very approximate guide to the routes taken by invaders. Trade routes probably followed the same lines as invasion routes and had considerable influence on the development of civilisation in the south-east.

Welsh Mts

Lincoln Edge

Cotswolds

Chilterns

ICKNIELD WAY

Salisbury Plain

HARROWAY

R. Rhine

R. Seine

Invaders from 2500-1700 BC
Invaders from 1900 BC
Iron Age invaders from 500 BC

ground over 300 ft.

| 0 | 50 | 100 | miles |
| 0 | 50 | 100 | 150 | kilometres |

1. BRITAIN BEFORE THE ROMANS

The island of Britain is situated at the edge of the Euro-Asian land mass. Throughout history it has been a refuge for those tribes who found the strength of their neighbouring tribes too much to oppose. The first people in Britain were hunters and food-gatherers who were followed, about 3,500 BC, by the settlers who first cultivated land. For many hundreds of years only the light, chalky soils on the downs and higher land were cultivated because suitable tools for tackling heavier soils were lacking.

Some time about 300 BC settlers from the area we now know as France arrived in Britain seeking homes. We call these people 'Marnians' because it was from the neighbourhood of the River Marne that they came. They were very fond of beautiful ornaments and were skilled craftsmen who could fashion even metals into wonderful objects. They were very fond of colour and their love of decoration greatly influenced the artistic work of the other settlers in Britain. However, these men had to move up country beyond the Humber River before they could find suitable land to settle. They formed the tribe of the Parisi.

In about 75 BC a new wave of settlers invaded Britain. These people, too, had their own culture. We call them 'Belgae' because they came from a part of France called *Gallia Belgica* by the Romans.

The Belgae applied their knowledge of iron and other metals not only in the creation of beautiful objects, but also in

This torc, or necklace (diameter 7½ in, 19 cm), was found at Snettisham in Norfolk. It was made, probably in the first century BC, of electrum, a mixture of gold and silver. The twisted bands of metal were springy enough to open out so that the chief could place it round his neck. The rings at the end are hollow.

making farm tools, especially a new kind of plough, that could break up the heavy clay soils of the valleys. It was then possible for some tribesmen to clear the heavily wooded valleys and settle there. The Belgic tribes took over control of the south-east of Britain except East Anglia.

Belgic tribes minted coins of the type used on the Continent and were obviously interested in trading with the Roman Empire. Hunting-dogs from Britain were much prized in the Empire and many slaves were sent to the mainland as well. In return, continental luxury goods were sold to the British chiefs.

The slaves who were exported probably were captured during inter-tribal wars. Even Belgic tribes fought each other. The tribe of Trinovantes had their capital at Camulodunum, which was very well placed for trade with the Continent, and the Catuvellauni wished to capture this town so that they could enjoy the benefits of the Roman trade. Although Caesar's attacks of 55 and 54 BC checked their rise to power, the Catuvellauni, under their chieftain, Cunobelinus, extended their control over the Trinovantes, Atrebates and Dobunni during the years following 10 BC. Some of the defeated chiefs fled to the Roman Empire, and others who stayed in Britain hoped that the Romans would come and end the rule of the Catuvellauni.

The names shown are Latin ones derived from Roman sources and refer to the distribution of tribes after the Roman invasion of AD 43. Regnenses ('the people of the king') probably refers to a collection of smaller tribes controlled by Cogidubnus, who was rewarded with this position because he aided the Roman cause at the time of the invasion. Cantiaci may also be a name for a group of small tribes.

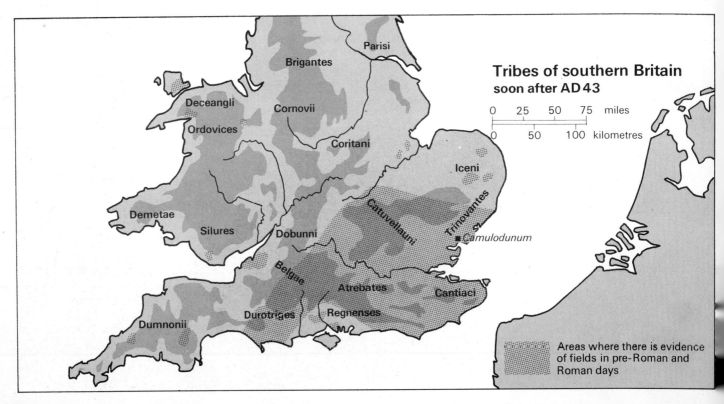

Tribes of southern Britain
soon after AD 43

0 25 50 75 miles
0 50 100 kilometres

Parisi
Brigantes
Deceangli
Ordovices
Cornovii
Coritani
Iceni
Demetae
Silures
Dobunni
Catuvellauni
Trinovantes
■ Camulodunum
Belgae
Atrebates
Cantiaci
Dumnonii
Durotriges
Regnenses

Areas where there is evidence of fields in pre-Roman and Roman days

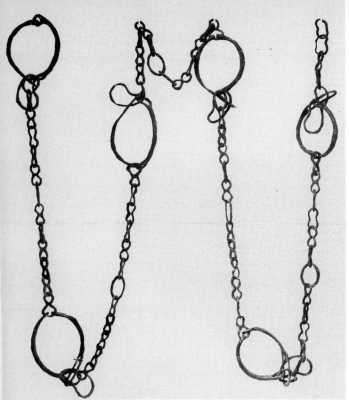

This coin, of the Iceni tribe, shows a horse and an ear of corn — both important things to the people. The coin, found at Honingham in Norfolk, is similar to the type minted in Gaul. (Three times the actual size.)

The Atrebates had Latin inscriptions on some of their coins. The word 'Rex' (King) is clearly visible. This type of coin is a copy of Roman coins. (Three times the actual size.)

This slave chain (length 13¼ ft, 4 m), found at Lords Bridge near Cambridge, was made to fit round the necks of six people. The slave trade between Britain and the Continent flourished both before and after the Roman invasion.

Roman model (length 2⅜ in, 6 cm) of a plough drawn by oxen. Although this model from Piercebridge in County Durham was made long after the Romans came to Britain, this kind of plough was used by some Britons from about 75 BC onwards. Notice the small size of the animals. Horses were considered too important to be used to pull ploughs.

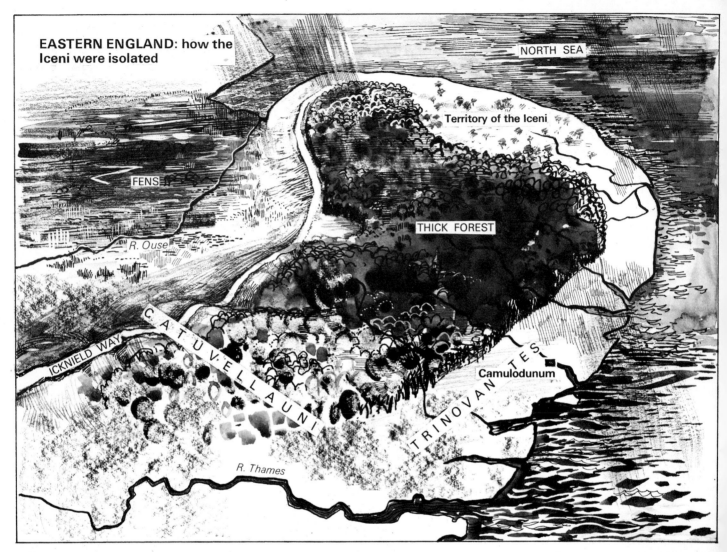

EASTERN ENGLAND: how the
Iceni were isolated

NORTH SEA

Territory of the Iceni

FENS

R. Ouse

THICK FOREST

ICKNIELD WAY

CATUVELLAUNI

TRINOVANTES

Camulodunum

R. Thames

The Iceni of Norfolk were not a Belgic tribe and were alarmed at the rise to power of the Catuvellauni. However, as the map above shows, dense woodland defended their southern boundary from Catuvellaunian attack while the terrible Fens prevented access from the west, and the North Sea to the north and east of them gave them a link with the Continent but did not help their British neighbours in any plans of invasion. The Iceni were virtually isolated, with only the Icknield Way – a ridge of higher, chalky ground, free from too many trees – as a way into their territory. Within their own lands they had some good grazing country, especially on the northern coastal fringe and on the boundary at the edge of the forest.

How the people lived

All the tribes of Britain were ruled in much the same sort of way. A chieftain, or king, had almost complete control along with a few powerful nobles, who were either his friends or rivals. Some of these kings and nobles hoped for Roman support, and others hated Roman influence.

These rich men made their lives more exciting by indulging in inter-tribal wars, when they would collect their followers together, dress up in fine clothes and ornate weapons, and raid the territory of their neighbours. Sometimes, as our picture shows, they went on wild boar hunts, which were also dangerous undertakings. Probably they hunted mostly on foot as horses were too valuable to risk in this form of sport. At such times the bravery of the hunting-dogs was almost as important as that of the men, because a wounded or cornered boar could inflict terrible wounds with its tusks.

Although the rich may have had exciting lives, the lives of the ordinary people were hard. Despite the fact that trade with the Roman Empire continued to grow before and after the invasion, it did not benefit the common man, who was a farmer.

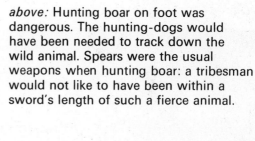

above: Hunting boar on foot was dangerous. The hunting-dogs would have been needed to track down the wild animal. Spears were the usual weapons when hunting boar: a tribesman would not like to have been within a sword's length of such a fierce animal.

left: Fields like these, on Smacam Down in Dorset, were used from pre-Roman times until the eighteenth century in many parts of Britain. They were usually about 33—44 yards (30—40 m) square, but some, on Belgic farms, were narrower, 130 yards (120 m) long. Even with the Belgic plough the furrows were shallow. The crops could not get deep roots and therefore did not thrive as they might otherwise have done.

This farmer would have been fairly well off. Many British homes were much poorer than this. Britons appear to have made frequent use of carts when moving around; the carts too would have been pulled by oxen and not horses. Trousers were useful when riding a horse, especially in cold weather. Note the lack of stirrups.

The tribes of the south-east cultivated land as well as raising stock. In their fields crops of turnip, cabbage, parsnip and grain were grown. Belgic farmers had the choice of three grain crops: wheat, spelt and barley. Usually the farmer could only grow enough to feed his family and pay his taxes, which were often collected in kind.

As you moved away from the south-east, cultivated lands disappeared and stock-breeding was the main form of farming practised.

The homes of the ordinary farmers were often made of wood and clay with a thatched roof. The fire was in the middle of the house and the smoke escaped through a hole in the roof. No doubt they could be dry and warm.

Chysauster village, Cornwall. Eight houses partly built of stone, each with its own courtyard, form this village which was occupied during the Roman period. Like most villages, it remained little influenced by Roman ideas.

The druids

The priests lived a different life from the nobles or peasant farmers. They looked after the temples, which were often enclosed in large fields. The priests were able to live comfortably on the sacrifices and offerings made to the gods and goddesses of the tribe. The priests were often asked by the nobles for advice on important matters and this gave them influence.

The gods and goddesses of one tribe were not necessarily the same as those of the next: so one tribe could not hope for support from another tribe on the grounds that they worshipped the same gods. Somehow or other the druids managed to be chief priests of all these religions and so they could get support from all of the tribes. In this respect at least they were more powerful than the chieftains.

We know very little about the druids, because they worked so secretly. Their religion was a cruel one that included human sacrifices, but these priests were men of intelligence and learning who influenced many people in the western part of the Roman Empire and beyond. They had great influence in Ireland, for example, which was never part of the Roman Empire. The Romans killed any druid they could find in an effort to end their influence.

An artist's idea of a British temple. The post-holes for the columns of this temple were found when workmen were clearing ground for a new runway at London (Heathrow) Airport. From this and other evidence, archaeologists built up a picture of what the temple site might have looked like.

2. THE LEGIONS COME

In the year AD 43 the Emperor Claudius sent Aulus Plautius with four legions to conquer Britain. These legions were: IInd Augusta, IXth Hispana, XIVth Gemina and XXth Valeria. The VIIIth Legion was held in reserve on the continent.

We do not really know why Claudius sent his legions. Perhaps he was after metal ore. He may have wanted a good corn-growing area or, perhaps, he thought a free Britain was a nuisance to the Empire. Maybe he only wanted to show that he could capture a country.

Many tribes, including the Iceni, welcomed the Romans or at least surrendered without a fight. Some tribes, including the Catuvellauni, fought the Romans. One by one these tribes were defeated. Claudius himself came over probably with part of the VIIIth Legion which stayed in Britain for a short time only. He accepted the surrender of some tribes. He then gave Aulus Plautius some vague instructions and went back to Rome, obviously content to leave the matter in the hands of the general.

The Romans continued to advance with most of the fighting going on in the west. Sometimes the Britons would defend hill forts.

We do not have a picture of Aulus Plautius but here is one of Vespasian who commanded the IInd Legion Augusta. This life-sized carving shows him as emperor 25 years later.

Opposite is a picture of Vespasian's legion attacking the hill fort of Maiden Castle in Dorset. Before assaulting, the Romans forced the defenders to take cover by firing stones and darts from their catapults (seen in the foreground). The arms of the catapult were held in place by ropes of hair or hide. When the ropes were twisted the catapult was tensioned. Vespasian and his staff officers directed the battle from a vantage point. As the Romans charged, the Britons hurled many sling-stones at them and the Romans raised their shields, perhaps forming a 'testudo'. Buildings outside the fort were burned down perhaps to cause fear in the defenders or to form a smoke screen.

left: This stone ($8\frac{1}{2} \times 14$ in, $21 \cdot 5 \times 36$ cm) was found on Hadrian's Wall. It is therefore of much later date than the invasion of AD 43 (the earliest possible date being AD 122). However, it shows the symbols of the IInd Legion Augusta: Capricorn (possibly representing the half-man, half-god, Pan) and Pegasus (the winged horse ridden, according to myth, by the heroes Perseus and Bellerophon). Both creatures face a standard of the legion which they guard.

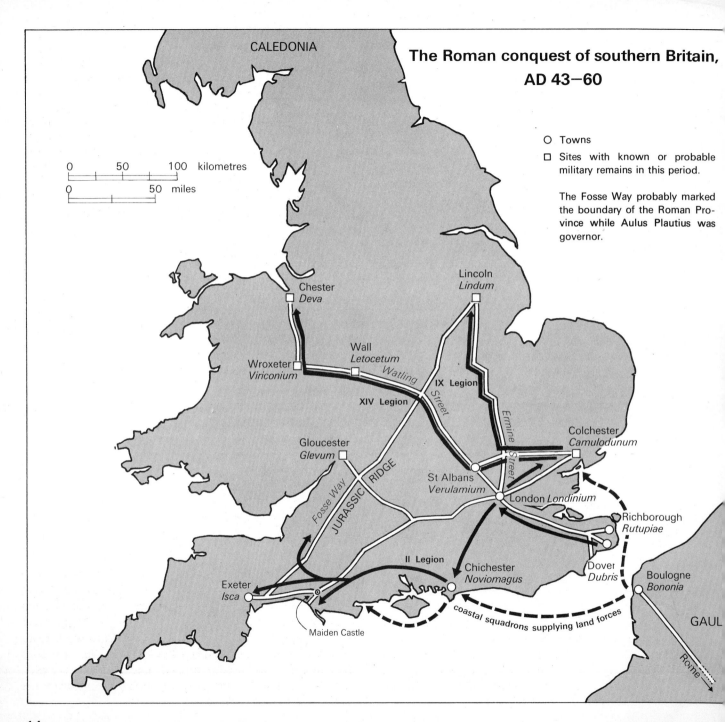

CALEDONIA

The Roman conquest of southern Britain, AD 43–60

0   50   100   kilometres

0   50   miles

O Towns

□ Sites with known or probable military remains in this period.

The Fosse Way probably marked the boundary of the Roman Province while Aulus Plautius was governor.

Lincoln
Lindum

Chester
Deva

Wall
Letocetum

Watling

IX Legion

Wroxeter
Viriconium

XIV Legion

Street

Ermine Street

Colchester
Camulodunum

Gloucester
Glevum

JURASSIC RIDGE

Fosse Way

St Albans
Verulamium

London *Londinium*

Richborough
Rutupiae

II Legion

Chichester
Noviomagus

Dover
Dubris

Boulogne
Bononia

Exeter
Isca

Maiden Castle

coastal squadrons supplying land forces

GAUL

Rome

In 1971 the eastern side of 'the Lunt' Roman fort at Baginton (near Coventry) was reconstructed. This outside view of the gateway shows the small ditch in front of the rampart, covered with turf to prevent erosion. The palisade, gates and gate tower are all of wood. Stone did not replace wood here as the fort was not occupied for long.

The Romans soon overran the south-east of Britain. Camulodunum (Colchester) became the capital of the province of Britain. The Romans also built a bridge over the River Thames and soon the trading town of Londinium (London) grew up on the spot. The Romans soon found that Londinium was even better placed than Camulodunum.

As the legions advanced they built roads. Everyone knows that these roads were the best that could be built at the time. They let the Roman army move very quickly.

The Roman army reached the Jurassic Ridge (see the map on page 14). Perhaps the Romans had now conquered all that they had wanted. They built a legionary fortress at Glevum (Gloucester) to protect one end of the frontier. At the other end a legionary fortress was built at Lindum (Lincoln). A road, called the Fosse Way, formed a link between the two bases and along this road were scattered smaller forts. However, the tribes beyond this line caused trouble and gradually the frontier was pushed forward.

Life in the new province

Behind the frontier all was peaceful. The Iceni were even allowed to keep their chief so long as they paid taxes to the Roman government. The Romans allowed them this privilege because the Iceni had become their allies. Besides, the Romans did not want the trouble of sending soldiers to the isolated lands of the Iceni.

Camulodunum, Londinium and Verulamium (St Albans) soon grew to be large towns – for those days.

Roman settlers had not yet moved into most of the province. Camulodunum was an exception to this rule. Here the Romans settled soldiers who had been retired from the legions in Britain. They were called 'veterans' and Camulodunum was given the important rank of 'colony'. Because Camulodunum was the capital of the province of Britain, a large temple was built there. It was made in the best Roman style and set in an area cut off from the rest of the town. This temple must have been visible from a long way off. People went there to worship 'the Spirit of the Emperor'. A large statue of Claudius was the main feature inside. The walls were decorated with marble and the cost of building the place must have been very high. The natives probably paid for all this.

The veterans needed land to grow crops and this was taken from the natives. The tribe that lived in this area was the Trinovantes.

The Catuvellauni also lost land when the Romans built Verulamium. This, like Camulodunum, was built as a model town to encourage the natives to live in towns as the Romans

below: Model of the temple of Claudius at Camulodunum, founded about AD 50. It was the largest Roman temple in Britain, the main building being about 39×30 yards (35× 27 m). Sandstone, alabaster, plaster mouldings and many foreign marbles were used in its construction. Colchester Keep, the largest in Britain, uses the base of the temple for foundations.

did. The regular plan of the town makes it very likely that the Roman army was used to build it. Probably the army had to supply the enormous quantities of wood needed. Nearly all the buildings were made of wood. A town like this was such a new idea in Britain that only the Roman army could have supplied the architects and craftsmen needed for the job.

Verulamium became the third largest town in Britain. Probably the land for Verulamium was taken away from the territory of the Catuvellauni. Around both Camulodunum and Verulamium, then, the native farmers suffered loss of land.

A bustling town also grew up quickly by the Thames bridge that the Roman army had built. This town, Londinium, was full of traders. It was in such a good position that the chief tax-collector of the province of Britain had his office there. The Romans called this man the 'procurator' and he had nearly as much power as the governor of the province because he was responsible for so much money.

The towns were a new, foreign innovation in the country, and only the people who wanted to live in them went there. The Romans hoped that lots of people would do so, and many did. In the countryside life went on much as before.

Plan of timber-framed shops at St Albans destroyed in AD 60. The room at the front opened on to the covered way which protected the shoppers in bad weather. The smaller room behind served as a working or living space. The windows would have had shutters but no glass as this was too expensive. Below is an artist's idea of the street scene.

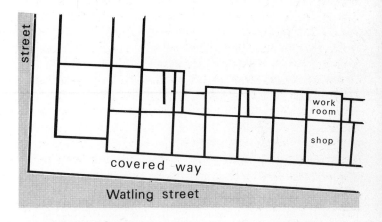

What the Britons and Romans thought of each other

Each Roman or Briton, of course, had his own idea of everybody else; but some ideas were shared by many. To the Roman soldiers, the Britons were the people who lived at the end of the world. They could not have feared them very much because many tribes had given up without a fight. For the same reason they could not have hated them fiercely.

The Romans would have been proud: proud that they had overcome the people at the end of the world so easily. Because they were proud, they would not have had much respect for the Britons.

The merchants who had come to Britain after the conquest hoped that there would be better markets for their goods. As we saw in the first chapter, Britons had traded with the Empire even before the invasion. Some of the merchants would have been honest and some dishonest: whichever the case, money was their chief concern.

The Roman governor of Britain hoped that the people would settle down quietly to Roman rule while he got on with the job of keeping the frontiers. Chiefs and nobles were encouraged to live in towns which were supposed to be the centre of tribal life under Roman rule. They were expected to be proud of their town and of the Roman Empire. They were not encouraged to be proud of Britain itself. The Romans built temples dedicated to the 'Spirits of the Place' and temples to the 'Spirit of Rome' are common throughout the Empire. The Romans hoped that by worshipping in these places the Britons would believe in the same ideals as the Romans themselves.

The Roman procurator of Britain had to make sure that people stayed settled down for another reason – it made it easier to collect taxes. Besides this, the richer the province grew the more money there was from taxes.

What did the Britons think of the Romans? We can be sure that not all of them found everything to their liking, but that is not to say that they hated the Romans. British society remained divided into nobles, peasants and priests.

The peasants had nothing much to lose by Roman rule. Their way of life was not changed: they simply changed one ruler for another and sometimes, as in the case of the Iceni, did not even do that. But any sharp increase in taxation or any extra hardship was likely to make them blame the new rulers, and when that happened the peasants would not be slow to seize their weapons if a leader came forward.

The nobles who had supported the Roman cause had lost their independence. However, they had something to make up for it; a new way of living. Most of them do not seem to have grumbled but perhaps they were a little afraid.

Only the priests, the druids, were united in hating the Romans. The Romans hated the druids just as much: druids were killed or else fled to the wilder parts of Britain and new priests took over sacred duties in the new temples.

The situation in Britain at this time seemed similar to that found in other newly conquered areas. The Romans could have seen no sign that a rebellion was about to erupt.

Fine mosaics, like this one at Fishbourne, where Cogidubnus, the 'king' of the Regnenses might have lived, were made on the Continent and then shipped to Britain. Perhaps the buyer of this mosaic paid for it by selling his slaves to a continental slave-dealer.

A large haul of arms.
The decorated weapons
belonged to those of some social position.

3. THE BRITONS ARE ANGERED

It seems as though the Britons had mixed feelings, though not many of them hated the Romans enough to risk their lives in a revolt. Any rebellion that had a chance of success would need support from all levels of society: nobles, peasants and priests. Also, a leader would have to be found. We are now going to look at the course of events that united all sections of society. To do this we need to go back to the years just after AD 43.

At first the tribe of Iceni must have been quite happy with the new situation that the Roman invasion had brought. The powerful tribe of Catuvellauni, who had threatened the Iceni, were not having a very easy time under their Roman masters. The Iceni, on the other hand, had kept their king and had an alliance with Rome.

But a rude shock awaited the Iceni and all those who thought the Romans had left them some measure of independence. Less than five years after the invasion they learned just how much their independence was worth.

The Roman governor, Ostorius Scapula, was having a tough job fighting in Wales. Caratacus, son of Cunobelinus, the king of the Catuvellauni, had fled to the Welsh hills when it became impossible for him to carry on fighting in southern Britain. Treachery brought about his capture by Ostorius Scapula in AD 50. But in the meantime the governor called for most of the troops stationed in Britain to help him. Of course, he dared not count on the tribes staying loyal to Rome and so he had all their weapons collected up – even the Iceni lost their weapons. The governor's men searched huts and asked awkward questions until they were satisfied that no weapons remained. Perhaps the war chariots were taken away, too, which would have annoyed the nobles.

A few of the Iceni were furious at this treatment and rose in revolt: only to be crushed by a single regiment of dismounted cavalrymen. It was after this that Ostorius Scapula founded the colony for ex-soldiers at Camulodunum. Perhaps he wanted these men to keep a watch on the local natives.

We have already written of how the building of Verulamium and Camulodunum forced many farmers to leave their lands. Some Britons stayed in the towns where they could farm or trade. The Romans did not seem too harsh at first. Those who moved away must have felt hatred of all townspeople, Romans and Britons alike. Sometimes a Roman ex-soldier who wanted land could simply trick the native into selling his farm, calling him a prisoner or slave as he did so. This added insult to injury. Perhaps many a Briton starved to death because his farm would have been his only source of food. As the ejected farmers moved away they spread stories of the cruelty of the Romans all around.

The town of Camulodunum housed many Britons who were thrilled by the town's theatre and the lifelike statues in the temples. The colony even had a senate modelled on the one in Rome. Other Britons living there felt differently. The Roman ex-soldiers were proud and cruel. Look how Facilis, a centurion of the XXth Legion gazes out from his tombstone: proud – even in death. See how Longinus' tombstone seems to say 'I've beaten Britons' as his horse tramples on an enemy. What would Britons who saw these tombstones have felt? Would they have admired the statue of Victory that the Romans set up in the town to celebrate their success?

The whole tribe of Trinovantes, whether they lived in Camulodunum or not, would have to pay for the expensive temple of the 'Spirit of the Emperor' and its upkeep. All the Trinovantes, nobles (who had lost power) and peasants (who had lost lands) and priests (who had lost jobs) joined in hating the Romans.

In AD 54 the Emperor Nero came to power in Rome. He had a lot of help in ruling the Empire from his tutor, Seneca. Seneca was a clever philosopher who is still famous for his writings but he was a rich man who intended to become richer.

A Briton is ordered off land that he once farmed. Such people faced starvation and had little to lose by rebelling.

The tombstone of Facilis, showing him in full dress armour. The vine-stick in his right hand was his symbol of power. As he died before AD 49 he was probably not a settler. Translated the inscription reads: 'Marcus Favonius Facilis, son of Marcus of the Pollian tribe, centurion of the XXth Legion. Erected by his freedmen Verecundus and Novicius. Here he lies.'

The tombstone of the cavalry officer Longinus who also died before the rebellion. He is shown triumphing over death as well as mortal foes. His face was deliberately smashed by the rebels. The inscription means: 'Longinus, son of Sdapezematycus, Duplicarius [officer] of the First Squadron of Thracian Cavalry, from the territory of Sardica. Aged forty in his fifteenth year of service. Erected by his heirs in accordance with his will. Here he lies.'

He poured money into the provinces in order to get high rates of interest. He even loaned money to the British tribes, including the Iceni and Trinovantes.

Borrowing money was a new idea to the Britons. As the Emperor Claudius had given gifts of money to some tribes, the tribesmen now thought that Seneca's loans must be much the same thing. They did not understand that the money was to be repaid, with interest.

The cost of keeping Britain was mounting all the time and Nero even thought of giving up the whole province but by AD 57 he had changed his mind. He finally decided to conquer more of Britain as he thought this would work out cheaper in the long run. But more money would be needed for the renewed efforts of the army. The money for further conquests in Britain had to be raised, partly at least, from those British tribes that the Romans ruled.

Catus Decianus was the man chosen to get this money by heavier taxes. He was sent to Britain as procurator. He behaved little better than a bandit and soon became the most hated Roman of all in the eyes of native Britons. Even as we look back over 1900 years we can find nothing good in the man: the best that can be said of him is that he was not the only one to blame for the rebellion of Boudicca and that his friends and officials were as bad as he was.

Suetonius Paulinus

In AD 58 Suetonius Paulinus was sent to Britain as governor. In the eyes of the people of the Roman world he was one of the best generals alive. He had fought in mountainous country before, so he was a good choice for the task of conquering Wales.

Suetonius set out to get victory, and from the first he applied his mind to the problems of the frontier. He had no time to enquire into the doings of Catus Decianus. The Roman government expected Suetonius and Decianus to keep an eye on each other to prevent dishonest behaviour. The basic idea of governor keeping watch on procurator, and procurator watching governor was used throughout the Empire. Sometimes it did not work. In Britain it was not working in AD 59.

Suetonius took the XIVth and XXth Legions to Wales and left the IInd Legion in the south-west and the IXth at Lindum to guard the frontier. He had great success and moved towards Anglesey where there were the headquarters of the druids' religion; it was also useful corn-growing land. If Suetonius captured Anglesey then North Wales would be in Rome's grasp.

Boudicca

The king of the Iceni at this time was Prasutagus. His wife's name was Boudicca, and they had two daughters. He must have seen difficult times ahead because when he died in this same year, AD 59, he left half his kingdom to Nero, in the hope that his wife and daughters could have the other half. Things worked out differently.

Catus Decianus declared that the whole kingdom belonged to Nero. He also declared that the money given by Claudius to the Iceni was only a loan and had to be repaid, with interest – at once. Then he set about enforcing his orders. His robber-like officials, joined by ex-soldiers and Romans out for plunder, pounced on the territory of the Iceni.

The estates of the nobles were seized and they themselves treated like slaves. The poor lost the little they had. Boudicca herself, who is supposed to have been bad-tempered, resisted the slaves of Decianus so they flogged her, and her daughters were assaulted.

The Britons began to hold secret meetings (see opposite). Nobles and peasants complained to one another about Catus Decianus and his taxes, about Roman colonists at Camulodunum and British 'traitors' who lived in the towns with the Romans. The priests joined in, too, when they knew that the headquarters of druidism were threatened.

The druids probably called on the Britons to rebel, and Boudicca herself had already decided that this was exactly what she would do. More meetings were held and Boudicca was chosen as leader. All types of people from a number of tribes had joined together and had found a leader. Nothing now could stop rebellion.

We do not have a picture of Boudicca but Cassius Dio, a Roman historian, said that: 'She was huge and frightening to look at with a mass of ginger hair that hung to her knees. Her voice was as harsh as her looks. She dressed in a multi-coloured tunic with a thick cloak fastened by a brooch flung over it, and wore a heavy gold necklace. She shook a spear to terrify all who watched her.'

The Menai Straits, looking north-east over Port Dinorwic and Anglesey. Suetonius' cavalry swam the straits somewhere near here while flat-bottomed boats carried the infantry across.

Chances of success

Boudicca had nothing to lose by rebellion and had many private wrongs to revenge. Her chances of success were high: she knew that the druids would support her. The Roman army in Britain was not as large as the army she hoped to have.

How many tribes joined Boudicca we do not know. Tacitus, another Roman historian, says that there were the Iceni, Trinovantes 'and others'. Cassius Dio says the rebel army was 120,000 strong – but that must have been an over-estimate. However, it was a very large army and Catus Decianus and his agents must have been very careless not to have found out what was going on – even if there were British 'secret agents' telling the people in the towns not to worry, that no trouble was coming.

Two attacks

Meanwhile, in the west, Suetonius stormed Anglesey. His cavalry swam across the Menai Straits and his legions followed in boats. A fierce battle raged. The druids were slain, their sacred altars smashed. Suetonius had met with complete success.

Then a messenger arrived: there was a serious rebellion in the province. Verulamium, the nearest important town, was more than 250 miles distant from Suetonius and his legions.

Anglesey
Mona

Chester
Deva

4. THE REBELLION

At the chosen moment, with Suetonius far away and the local population living quietly, a furious mob burst from the wooded lands of the Iceni, out for revenge and plunder. Boudicca, at their head, made a speech (according to Dio), calculated to make them more frenzied than ever: 'Don't fear the Romans,' she bellowed, 'they protect themselves with helmets, breast-plates and greaves. They provide themselves with walls and palisades and trenches. Why do they adopt such methods of fighting? Because they are afraid. We prefer rough and ready action . . . Our tents are safer than their walls. Our shields protect us better than their suits of mail . . . Let us show them that they are hares and foxes trying to rule dogs and wolves.'

As the yelling mob surged forward, burning and plundering pro-Roman settlements, their numbers grew. The Trinovantes joined in and the horde descended on Camulodunum. Even as they came the colonists could not decide what to do, so they appealed to Catus Decianus for help. This man, the highest civil official in the province, sent only 200 men. The town was seized with panic. The superstitious people believed the story that the statue of Victory in Camulodunum had fallen down with its back to the enemy as if it was running away.

'Delirious women chanted of destruction at hand', wrote Tacitus. 'They cried that in the local senate-house outlandish yells had been heard; the theatre had echoed with shrieks; at the mouth of the Thames a ghost settlement had been seen in ruins. A blood-red colour in the sea, too, and shapes like human corpses left behind by the tide.' Paralysed by indecision which was doubtless made worse by different rumours the colonists failed to build any defences and seem to have trusted to the temple to provide them with a strong refuge. They did not even send away the women and children to safety.

As Boudicca's horde crashed through the suburbs, the terrified defenders looked out from the temple. They saw, a quarter of a mile away to the west, on the ridge that dominated the town, flames and smoke pouring from all the buildings. There was no thought of plunder, the mob simply fired shops complete with goods: goods imported from the hated Empire.

St Albans
Verulamium

Colchester
Camulodunum

London
Londinium

Imagine the thoughts of a veteran soldier who, knowing how he had ill-treated the natives, saw them charging down from the ridge towards the temple; with flames and smoke of the ruined town as a backcloth. He could expect no mercy; neither could any defender in the temple. For two days the colonists held off the mob. Then the natives broke in. They slew soldiers, colonists, women, old people, slaves and children alike: no one was left alive. Finally the temple of Claudius itself was pulled to the ground and the statue of the Emperor smashed to fragments. Somewhere else in the town rebels found another life-sized statue of Claudius and wrenched the metal head from the metal body and carried it away, finally to fling it into the River Alde. You can see a picture of this head on page 46.

Petilius Cerealis, the young commander of the IXth Legion stationed with half his men at Longthorpe (near Peterborough), or perhaps near Lindum (Lincoln), heard of the rebellion. He decided that it must be put down straight away before it could grow. He gathered a mixed force of legionaries and cavalry and set off southwards down Ermine Street (see the map on page 14). Somewhere along the way a large force of natives lay in wait. They pounced and cut Cerealis' force to pieces: only Cerealis and the cavalry managed to fight their way free and retreat to Lindum, leaving more than 1000 legionaries dead. For the time being the IXth Legion was finished as a fighting force. Any Roman forces surviving in the south-east must have been virtually besieged in their posts. Jubilation gripped the rebels.

Nothing stood between them and the unwalled towns of Londinium and Verulamium.

The capture of Camulodunum and the destruction of Cerealis' force were two big victories for the rebels. The whole rebellion had been successful up to this point and the rebels had shown excellent generalship. It is possible that Boudicca herself was responsible for all the planning, but she must have had good military advisers, because she could not have been leading the attack on Camulodunum and on Cerealis' force at almost the same time. On the other hand Boudicca might have only been the chief member of a group of generals who planned the rebellion or perhaps only a 'figure-head'. Whoever the real 'brain' was, the rebels massed for their attack on the civil population of the Romanised areas.

In Londinium itself, Catus Decianus, 'public enemy number one' to the rebels, gave up hope. The cowardly man did not even organise the evacuation of women and children to the friendly tribe of the Regnenses, but bundled his goods, personal friends and staff on to a ship, deserted his post, and fled to the Continent.

Londinium was already a port of some size by AD 60. No doubt when Decianus fled some Britons fled too. Perhaps some escaped over the Thames in small boats similar to the ones shown in the foreground. Notice that the buildings are wooden: Londinium was still a new town.

Suetonius returns from Wales

Furious at the turn of events, which had robbed him of the glory that the conquest of Anglesey should have given him, Suetonius Paulinus did not lose his judgement. Although he had the fine fighting force of the XIVth and XXth Legions with him he was hopelessly far away from the scene of action: the IXth Legion had been defeated and only the IInd Legion was within reasonable distance of Londinium. Sending an order for that legion to meet him on the way, Suetonius set off at the head of a cavalry force galloping through the valleys of North Wales and into the Midlands to join Watling Street. He arrived at the place where he expected the IInd Legion to meet him. It was not there!

What had happened was this: the commander of the IInd Legion was away from his unit and it was commanded by the praefectus castrorum, Poenius Postumus. When this man received the order to march he failed to obey it. We do not know why. The local tribe, the Silures, were causing trouble and Postumus may have thought he should stay to hold them down.

So Suetonius had another difficult choice; was he to wait until the XIVth and XXth Legions caught up with him or not? No one knew what exactly was happening in Londinium or how large the rebel force was. Sooner or later someone would have to go on a reconnaissance – you could not march an army into a completely unknown situation – and Suetonius thought it might as well be him. So off he raced with his cavalry down the long, direct route to Londinium, the road we call Watling Street. It was extremely dangerous. The whole area might be swarming with rebel bands. Even if he reached Londinium, Suetonius risked being trapped in the town.

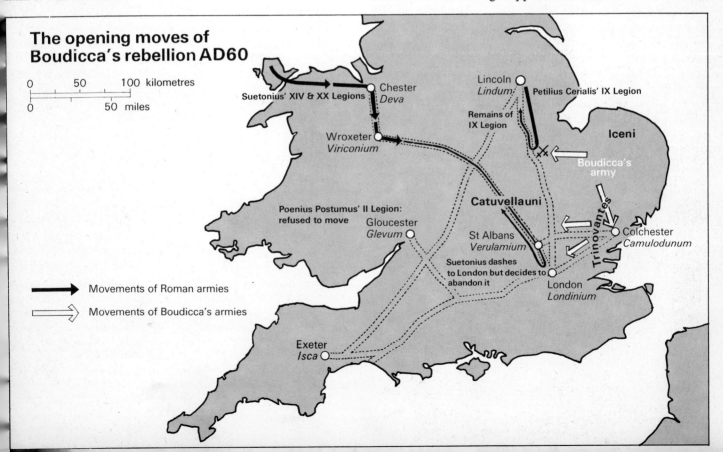

The opening moves of Boudicca's rebellion AD60

0   50   100 kilometres

0   50 miles

Suetonius' XIV & XX Legions

Chester
Deva

Lincoln
Lindum

Petilius Cerialis' IX Legion

Remains of
IX Legion

Iceni

Wroxeter
Viriconium

XX

Boudicca's
army

Catuvellauni

Poenius Postumus' II Legion:
refused to move

Gloucester
Glevum

St Albans
Verulamium

Colchester
Camulodunum

Trinovantes

Suetonius dashes
to London but decides to
abandon it

London
Londinium

→ Movements of Roman armies

⇨ Movements of Boudicca's armies

Exeter
Isca

After a hard ride Suetonius and his exhausted force reached Londinium. The situation was worse than he had expected. There was no one to give him reliable details – Catus Decianus and his staff had fled – and no chance of holding the town against a large army. If Londinium fell, then Suetonius' link with the Continent would be broken and no reinforcements could be brought directly to the scene of action.

'Eventually,' says Tacitus, 'the small size of his force . . . decided him to abandon the city of Londinium.' The people pleaded with him not to go, but he had made up his mind. Able-bodied men were allowed to go with him but the rest – old people, women and children – had to be left; the rebels were closing in and Suetonius just did not have enough men to cover an organised evacuation. Perhaps some managed to escape to the territory of the Regnenses, but when Suetonius left to rejoin his army he left most of the inhabitants of Londinium to their fate.

Boudicca was not having an easy task, either. Although the rebels had been successful, success had gone to their heads. Boudicca found it harder to control them: despite the large numbers of her force she had failed to catch Suetonius as he sped to Londinium, failed to trap him in Londinium and failed to stop him when he went to rejoin his army. Because of this the whole rebellion was to change its course.

Whatever Boudicca and her generals may have thought, the rebels were more than satisfied with the path events had taken. Everything they had set out to achieve had been accomplished: the colonists of Camulodunum were dead, the hated temple of the spirit of Claudius destroyed and Catus Decianus had been driven from the province with all his staff. On top of this they had defeated the IXth Legion and now the largest towns in the province lay wide open to attack. Which would they attack first? Londinium had housed the hated procurator and was the largest town in the province, full of traitors, merchants and money-lenders who had come to swindle the people. Verulamium, on the other hand, was a showpiece of the Roman government. Claudius had given it an important position. Fine buildings had been put up with the help of the army: as we have seen, shops even had covered pavements in front of them. In it lived many Britons who had adopted Roman ways; 'traitors' in the eyes of the rebels, living on land seized by the Romans from the Catuvellauni (and there must have been many of this tribe in Boudicca's army).

Watling Street, a typically direct Roman road, looking south-east from Hockliffe, Bedfordshire. Roman armies could move quickly along such roads. Wherever Roman armies went the soldiers built roads. However, Suetonius would not have seen such well-ordered fields and housing as this photograph shows; most of the land was uncultivated in his day. Also, the surface of the road would have been of gravel and not tarmac.

Two cities destroyed

We do not know whether Londinium or Verulamium was attacked first or if they were both attacked by different parts of Boudicca's horde. What we do know is that when the rebels stormed Londinium, the area between where St Paul's and the Bank of England now stand was filled with flame, smoke, the screams of tortured and dying inhabitants and the victorious yells of the rebels. The heads of the murdered townspeople were flung into the Thames or the Walbrook and the bodies left to rot in the smouldering heap of ruins. The same scenes were enacted at Verulamium, amid the flames of the wooden shops and houses. Many women were taken to the groves of trees sacred to the goddess Andrasta and tortured to death. The purpose of this (if there was one) was to make it impossible for any rebel to be pardoned by the Roman government. This was to be a merciless struggle: victory or death.

The destruction of these towns with the attending horrors of the 'gallows, fire and the cross' (Tacitus' words) was the worst disaster to have befallen a civil population in the Roman Empire for a very long time. Tacitus tells us that in a few weeks the three largest towns of the province had been destroyed and about 70,000 people had been killed.

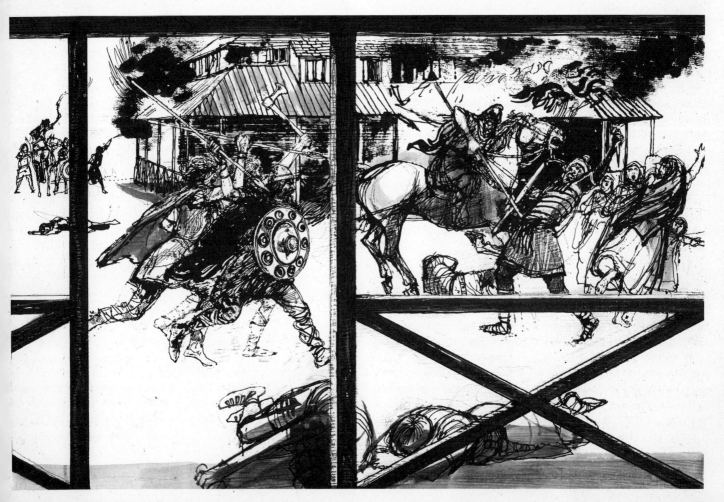

5. THE ROMANS STRIKE BACK

Leaving the ruins of his province behind him, Suetonius had retreated north-westwards, and somewhere in the Midlands rejoined his army. The IInd Legion still had not moved from its camp and Suetonius could not take all of the XIVth and XXth Legions with him, as some troops were needed to guard the frontier in North Wales. Some troops from the XXth Legion, therefore, were left behind to protect this border; probably they were stationed at Deva (Chester). It was also necessary for Suetonius to guard the rest of the frontier: both the Silures and Brigantes might join the rebellion. Suetonius did not have much choice as to which units to leave on guard. The IInd Legion could keep the Silures in check; anyway Suetonius now probably thought it untrustworthy and did not want it in his army. The remnants of the IXth Legion acted as a token force to watch the Brigantes.

Two armies prepare

In order to bring his army up to 10,000 men, Suetonius took auxiliary soldiers from other duties and placed them with his legions. As he had no sure supply route to the Continent, and could not get food from the area held by the rebels, Suetonius must have been anxious about how long his provisions would last. Because of this he would want to fight the decisive battle quickly. As he was heavily outnumbered, it was vital for him to fight on ground of his own choosing.

Boudicca also, in all probability, had similar problems. We do not know in which season the revolt occurred, but her warriors could not carry on their peacetime farming occupations during the revolt and so either they had not sown crops, or the crops were left unattended. In either case her army would be short of food. Boudicca might, possibly, have thought that this was good policy. Her army would have to fight the Roman forces and capture their bases, which were often well stocked with food, if the rebels did not want to be underfed in winter. Furthermore, Boudicca's army was so large that it would have been a problem to feed them at any time. If the fighting was over by winter then the force could split up and each man could look after himself.

From a military point of view Boudicca would want to see Suetonius defeated before he could get reinforcements. She must have known how highly the Romans rated his generalship. Such a man was dangerous with 10,000 soldiers and if he got more men it would be impossible to defeat him.

Boudicca's force was full of confidence. It was, perhaps, ten times the size of the Roman army and had enjoyed one great success after another since the start of the rebellion. But if there was a long delay before the fight with the Romans came, such a force might well cool down or become impatient or even mutinous because many were not skilled fighters.

The armies meet

The two armies moved towards each other. If you could look back to those times you would see the huge snake of the rebel army moving slowly but surely along. Every now and then a wagon loaded with women and children would get in the way of progress, but there was no thought of leaving them behind: everyone had to see the final battle. It would have been a noisy scene, too.

The Roman army was far better ordered and so moved much

quicker. The companies of men marched in blocks to a regular pace with centurions behind, making sure that no one slacked. There would have been no joyous cries among the Roman troops. They were on their own in a foreign, hostile country.

If we look only at the numbers on each side it is obvious that the Britons should have won. However, the Roman army was a disciplined, highly skilled force. The crack troops of this army were the legionaries and we have below a drawing of one of these to show you how he was armed. He carried two heavy javelins. Even if they did not hit an enemy soldier they might stick in his shield: with a javelin stuck in his shield, the enemy

could hardly use it and would be at a serious disadvantage. The legionary carried his sword on his right side. After throwing his javelins, when drawing the sword, he used his left hand to hold the scabbard steady and so his shield would automatically be brought across in front of his body. The short stabbing sword was easier to use in a confined space than a long one, and at really close quarters he had a large metal bump (boss) in the middle of his shield to knock over his enemy. The lower part of his body was free of armour to let him move easily, and so were his arms, but his head and the upper parts of his body were well covered.

A Roman legionary (*left*) and a British chieftain. Romans were short people but well armed. The legionary was a regular soldier who took pride in the achievements of his legion. Although he looked more colourful than the legionary, the British chieftain had less armour than the ordinary Roman infantryman and his weapons were less satisfactory. The chieftain's followers were even more poorly armed and often had no armour at all.

So much for the legionary. Boudicca's men mostly had no armour but carried shields to protect themselves. Only the richest could afford helmets and swords. A spear was the most usual weapon but no doubt there were knives, bows and arrows and even farm tools as well.

One of our pictures shows a reconstruction of a chariot. The Britons were famous for these war-machines but when the Romans disarmed the province the chariots were probably taken away too, so that we do not know whether or not Boudicca used many, though Dio says she had some.

The two armies probably met somewhere along the line of Watling Street. We do not know exactly where. Suetonius chose to line up his men at the mouth of a narrow valley. The sides of the valley were covered with trees and there were also thick woods behind Suetonius. This prevented the enemy from surrounding the Roman forces. In the centre of his battle line were the legionaries, probably in three blocks. The men stood fairly close together with their shields forming a defensive line across their chests. No doubt each man drew comfort from the friends on either side of him. Suetonius then ordered the auxiliary infantry to take up positions by the sides of the

below: British chariots were lightly built for speed and ease of movement. They were pulled by horses and the charioteer could run along the centre-shaft. The other man in the chariot was always a warrior who would either fight from the chariot or jump down from it and fight on foot, leaping aboard again should he need to retreat. However, such tactics seldom upset well-trained legionaries. This model is based on the remains of a chariot found in a bog on Anglesey.

This helmet and shield are of a kind used around the time of the rebellion though the Britons had no uniform as such. The bronze helmet with its ornamental horns was probably more of an encumbrance than a protection. The shield, also of bronze, was more useful being just over 1 metre long. Originally the bronze had a backing of leather or wood, and a decoration of a conventionalised boar was riveted to the front (the shield on page 31 is based on this one).

The picture opposite shows how, according to Tacitus, the two armies faced one another.

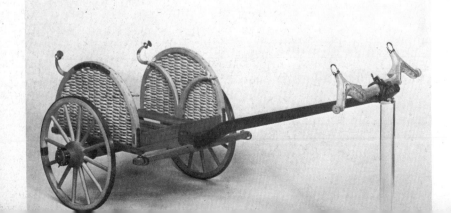

cavalry auxiliaries legionaries auxiliaries cavalry

Britons

This marble was carved 200 years after Boudicca's rebellion; but it shows the jumble of fighting and dying men which is typical of a hand-to-hand battle. Amongst other things a Roman trumpeter is shown and another Roman is grabbing his enemy's beard.

legions. Beyond the auxiliaries, on their outer flanks, the cavalry were massed in two groups.

The Britons longed to get to grips with the enemy and felt certain of success. The Romans appeared to be trapped with the rebels massed in front of them. Just like the Romans, the Britons wanted people around them whom they knew and trusted. Each Briton stood with his own tribe's forces. The rebels were so sure of victory that they brought their wives and children along to see the fun. In order to give them a better view, the wagons of the rebels were lined up behind the army for the women to stand on.

With both armies ready, the commanders gave short encouraging speeches: Boudicca, in Tacitus' words, cried 'The Romans will not even be able to stand up to the yells and din of our thousands, let alone the force of our charge. Look how few you are fighting! Remember why you are fighting and you will win the battle!'

Suetonius, who trusted his men's bravery and training, barked, 'Keep together; throw your javelins; strike with the bosses of your shields, and carry on from there! Don't give a thought to booty: win the victory, and you have got the lot.'

The battle

Suetonius gave the signal for battle, but hordes of rebels came yelling towards the legions. The legionaries balanced their javelins, with their left feet slightly forward for a greater effort and at 30 yards range hurled them. Up went the British shields. Javelins thudded deep into these and their soft iron necks bent. Unable to withdraw the twisted javelins, and pushed by shouting comrades from behind, many Britons threw away their useless shields. A second volley of javelins came, and at shorter range destruction was greater. However, the Britons pressed on towards the legionaries. The hideous clamour of human shouts and shrieks was now joined by the roar of iron meeting iron. Pushing and shoving, the opponents sought to knock each other over. A heavy spear thrust penetrated Roman armour, or a jab with a sword brought a Briton screaming to his knees before he was either despatched by a second Roman thrust, or trampled on by the pushing, heaving throng of Britons.

The anxious generals, Suetonius and Boudicca, looked on, giving fresh orders now and then. To the fighting men all was

Roman soldiers on board ship. The Romans had no reserve army and the reinforcements needed in Britain were drawn from the forces on the Rhine and transported across the North Sea. This bireme, a warship with two banks of oars, also carries a forward fighting tower.

confusion and danger. The smell of blood and sweat from tiring bodies was added to the din of battle. Only the lines of Roman soldiers showed any sign of order.

Slowly but surely, Suetonius saw his men get the upper hand, and at the right moment ordered the advance. With victorious shouts the legionaries, auxiliaries and cavalry burst forward in wedge formation. The Britons found the swords of the Romans darting like snakes' tongues as the legionaries advanced. They began to panic as it seemed more and more impossible to find ways of piercing the Romans' armour. Roman cavalry, with lances extended, swept round the sides of groups of Britons, pinning them together.

At last the Britons broke and fled. The wagons, on which were their own wives and children, got in their way. Held up by this obstacle the fleeing Britons were easy prey for the Romans. Drunk with success, every Roman soldier killed everything British that he came to: men, women, children and baggage animals. Corpses began to pile up: any effort at defence was useless. 'Heaps of dead!' wrote Tacitus, 'Just like the good old days! Some people thought that 80,000 Britons had been killed.'

Boudicca, with fugitive Britons running from the battle all around her, went away and poisoned herself. 'The Britons mourned her deeply', wrote Dio.

Suetonius took stock of Roman losses. Only 400 dead and just over that number wounded. It must have given him grim satisfaction. By keeping calm at the most crucial moments, he and his army had turned the tide of the rebellion.

The news of the victory quickly spread to all Roman forts. When Poenius Postumus heard it he was full of shame: he had disobeyed his governor and army regulations and prevented the IInd Legion from taking part in the victory. He drew his sword, placed the point on his chest and fell on it, stabbing himself to death.

Although Suetonius had gained a massive victory, the rebellion was not finished. Each tribe continued to fight on its own. They were scared to surrender to Suetonius.

Suetonius kept his army ready for action, while Nero sent reinforcements: 2000 legionaries sailed across the North Sea from the Rhine frontier to bring the IXth Legion back to full strength. Eight cohorts of auxiliaries, about 4000 men, were also sent over, and two cavalry regiments, about 1000 men.

Winter was coming on and the troops were given quarters in forts or camps with huts instead of tents. The main army was kept together while the auxiliaries and cavalry spread out over the rebellious tribes' lands. Everywhere famine gripped the miserable remnants of the rebellion. Many must have died of hunger and cold and despair. Nevertheless peace did not return.

While Suetonius and his army were getting their revenge, and crushing the revolt at the same time, the government at Rome sent out a new procurator: Julius Alpinus Classicianus.

Classicianus set about the problem of restoring civil rule but almost at once he made a dismaying discovery; the harsh methods used by Suetonius were ruining the province – if this went on there would be no people or property to tax.

Suetonius soon had arguments with Classicianus. Tacitus even says that the procurator urged the rebels to hold out until a new governor came. Probably this story is not true; Tacitus was on Suetonius' side. Classicianus wrote to Nero, 'There is no hope of ending the fighting until a governor to replace Suetonius is sent out.'

To Suetonius' anger, Nero sent Polyclitus, an ex-slave, to report at first hand on the situation in Britain. This official returned to Rome with his report. It confirmed what Classicianus had said. But Suetonius was a victorious general, and Nero had to wait for an excuse to remove him. Shortly after, some ships under Suetonius' command were wrecked and their crews drowned. So he was recalled to Rome though of course the real reason was that he was prolonging the rebellion. A new governor, Publius Petronius Turpilianus, was sent to Britain.

Winter brought no relief to the Britons. Unlike the warmly clad Roman legionaries, the fugitive rebels had little food or clothing to save them from the threat of death by exposure.

This undated tombstone of Lovesius had the initials 'V.V.' after the name of his legion – the XXth. The expanded text reads: 'G[aius] Lovesius Cadarus, of the tribe Papiria, of Emerita, soldier of the XXth Legion Valeria Victrix, aged 25 years, served 8. Frontinius Aquilo, his heir had this erected.'

6. REBIRTH

Clearing up

The new governor and procurator had very difficult tasks. The Roman government must have been watching the actions of both men carefully. The legions in Britain would be comparing Turpilianus with Suetonius, while the native population would be suspicious of everything Classicianus did.

We know exceedingly little of the work of these two men. We only know what Tacitus wrote about them, and as he sympathised with Suetonius, he is not likely to have given the new men the credit they deserved.

Some of the rebels kept on fighting, but they had no leader, with Boudicca dead. If there were other generals they could not manage to re-form the rebel army. The rebellion was clearly doomed. Even the fierceness had probably been lessened by the departure of Suetonius, feared for his stern measures.

Turpilianus and his legions put an end to the fighting. He had to keep law and order – it was part of his job. However, after two years his task was done and Turpilianus went back to Rome. Nero rewarded him with a Triumph: a procession given to victorious generals. The XIVth and XXth Legions were awarded the title *Victrix* (Victorious) for their gallant efforts during the rebellion.

Classicianus did as much work as Turpilianus. The unfairness of the previous tax-officials and the destruction that followed Suetonius' victory must have made the problems greater. Classicianus had understood the situation from the first, but could do little until Turpilianus arrived. He set to work.

Tax-collectors had to be found and a new list of property made in order to work out the amount of money that the taxes should bring in. No doubt Britain produced little wealth during this period, as everyone was unsettled and much property had been destroyed. Many of the merchants were dead and few new ones would have come from the Continent. Roman investors and traders would rather have given their attention to the provinces unaffected by the rebellion.

We may guess that large numbers of Britons would have

found it impossible to pay their taxes. Perhaps loans of money were made to people who needed it. This would help to get the province going, but there was a danger. Classicianus knew that the greed of Roman money-lenders had been a cause of the rebellion.

While engaged on this difficult work Classicianus died. His death must have delayed the work of reconstruction still further. He was buried in Londinium and his tombstone can be seen today in the British Museum. The words on it mean: 'To the shades of the dead: C. Julius Fabius Alpinus Classicianus . . . procurator of the Province of Britain. Set up by his wife Julia Pacata Indiana daughter of Indus.'

See how many of these words you can identify on our photograph. This is the only inscription we have in Britain about someone who actually played a part in Boudicca's rebellion.

A peaceful pause

No one seems to know the names of the next procurators of Britain, but they did fine work. The tax system appears to have begun to work smoothly. The towns made the procurator's job a little easier because it was more simple to organise tax-collecting in towns than in the countryside.

We do know the names of the governors who followed Turpilianus. In AD 63 Trebellius Maximus came. He stayed in office for six years, which is twice as long as a normal governorship lasted. This was probably because Nero decided that Britain needed stability. 'He governed the province like a gentleman', wrote Tacitus. Trebellius fought no wars and during six years in Britain people must have got to know what he was like. His extra-long stay helped the people to regain confidence. The man who followed Trebellius was Vettius Bolanus and likewise he let the province get on peacefully. Civil wars raged in the Roman Empire and Bolanus did well in keeping Britain quiet and free from this fighting. Bolanus stayed until AD 71 when the civil wars ended.

These nine years were of great importance for Britain. During them the province returned to normal life. It had achieved this after having suffered almost total disruption at the hands of Boudicca's rebels.

right: An antefix (or tile from a roof eave) showing the wild boar emblem of the XXth Legion. The probable date is second century. The legion remained in Britain throughout the Roman occupation. Agricola was its commander during the governorship of Cerealis.

Pieces of the tomb of Classicianus were found in different places in London. As the wording on Roman tombs was very formalised, it is possible to supply some of the missing letters from what we know of complete inscriptions. The tomb would have been about 8 ft (2·4 m) long.

The conquerors return

The new emperor after the civil wars was Vespasian, who had been a general during the invasion of Britain. As governor of Britain he sent out Petilius Cerealis. (Do you remember where he was during the rebellion?) Cerealis found the province quiet. It was safe to move forward again. He set out to conquer the Brigantes, the tribe which was believed to be the largest in the island of Britain. The governor who came after Cerealis, Julius Frontinus, conquered the powerful Silures. Agricola, governor from AD 78 to 85, successfully carried Roman arms to many parts of northern Britain. These men found the task hard, but the south-east of the island remained peaceful, even when Agricola recaptured the island of Anglesey. With the frontier pushed well away from them, the tribes of the south-east enjoyed over 300 years of almost uninterrupted peace.

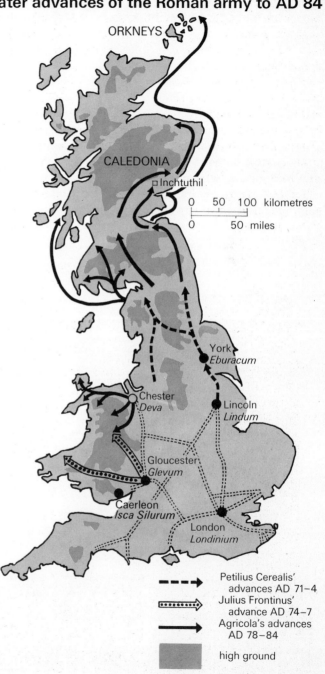

Later advances of the Roman army to AD 84

ORKNEYS

CALEDONIA

□ Inchtuthil

0   50   100 kilometres
0   50 miles

York
Eburacum

Chester
Deva

Lincoln
Lindum

Gloucester
Glevum

Caerleon
Isca Silurum

London
Londinium

- - - ➤ Petilius Cerealis'
advances AD 71–4
·····➤ Julius Frontinus'
advance AD 74–7
——➤ Agricola's advances
AD 78–84

high ground

7. ROMAN BRITAIN

Although we feel fairly certain about what happened in Britain after Boudicca's rebellion, we can only guess how far it was the rebellion that actually caused these things to happen.

The horrors of the rebellion had left their mark. The people who had suffered in it would have retained a sense of fury and pain for many years. Gradually, though, the bitterness must have died down and then both sides may have learnt a lesson. The Britons had learnt that it was impossible to throw the Romans out of Britain. You have already read how the Romans tried to treat their province more reasonably than they had done before the rebellion. Part of their policy was to make the Roman way of life appealing to the local noblemen. They did this by encouraging these chieftains to live in towns, and then to live more like the Romans themselves.

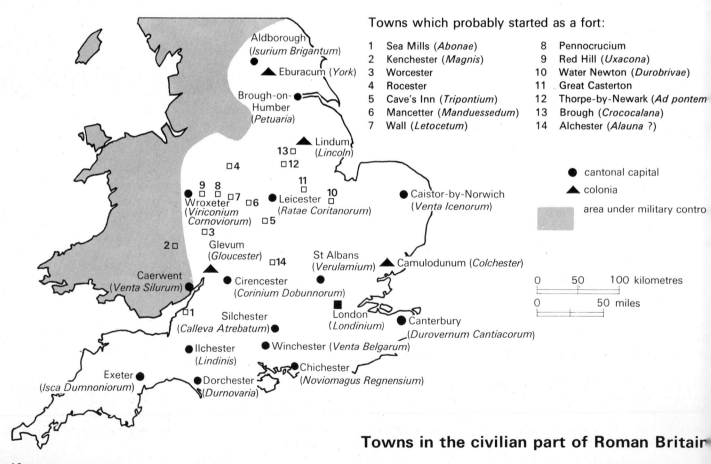

Towns which probably started as a fort:

1	Sea Mills (*Abonae*)	8	Pennocrucium
2	Kenchester (*Magnis*)	9	Red Hill (*Uxacona*)
3	Worcester	10	Water Newton (*Durobrivae*)
4	Rocester	11	Great Casterton
5	Cave's Inn (*Tripontium*)	12	Thorpe-by-Newark (*Ad pontem*)
6	Mancetter (*Manduessedum*)	13	Brough (*Crococalana*)
7	Wall (*Letocetum*)	14	Alchester (*Alauna ?*)

● cantonal capital

▲ colonia

▨ area under military control

0   50   100 kilometres

0   50 miles

Towns in the civilian part of Roman Britain

Life in the towns

There were many towns in Roman Britain, although some were more important than others. The map shows you where they were. Most of them were in the southern part of Britain. Many of these towns began as villages built beside forts, and they grew into towns after the Roman army had moved north.

In the towns there was law and order. The most important building in a town was its basilica, situated in the main square. This building was the equivalent of a town hall and law courts combined. There was comfort too; heated baths for the use of the citizens could be found in many towns. Naturally, there were shops which were convenient for the townsfolk and provided jobs for the craftsmen who made the goods for sale.

This painting shows how London may have appeared about AD 100. Notice the regular roads which were typical in Roman towns. The bridge across the Thames gave London much of its importance. There are no town walls, as Britain was peaceful at this time.

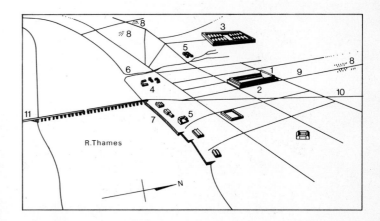

1	Basilica	7	Wharves
2	Forum	8	Cemeteries (outside the town)
3	Fort at Cripplegate	9	Road to York
4	Governor's Palace	10	Road to Colchester
5	Baths	11	Road to Chichester
6	Walbrook		

Here are some photographs of some objects it was possible to buy in the shops of Roman Britain. Pottery was, of course, of prime importance. The second-century vase (opposite) showing a gladiatorial fight between Memnon and Valentinus was something special but more ordinary ware is found in great abundance on many Roman sites. We give gifts to each other on special occasions; and so did the Romans. The lamp shown here is a New Year's present. Glassware was sometimes of local make but much was imported, especially from the Roman parts of Germany.

The goods sold were often made within the town itself. There was a factory for making glassware at Caistor by Norwich, and one for extracting silver from lead at Silchester, and many others. The two examples just quoted are small affairs; but larger ones did exist. There are the remains of a very large bakery in London and some of the potters' factories in Colchester must have been fairly large. On the opposite page you can see how the pottery was made. Usually the kilns were situated outside the town boundaries.

A wealthy Briton living in Roman style in a town had a comfortable life.

left: An oil lamp found near Ely bearing the greeting 'Annum Novum Favstum Felicem Mihi' literally, 'I wish myself a Happy New Year.' More probably, this was a gift to the whole household. The winged figure of Victory is surrounded by coins and nuts. Length about 4¾ in (12 cm).
below left: Glass vases of late second or early third century AD from Roman cemeteries near Cambridge. Glass, pottery and other objects were often buried with the dead in Roman times.
below: A third-century pewter jug (height 12 in, 30·5 cm) from Swavesey Cambridgeshire.

left: A pottery kiln ready for firing. This cut-away drawing shows the stoke-hole for the fire and the flues in the floor and roof for the escape of the hot gases. A vigorous up-draught is required for a high temperature. By regulating the amount of air entering the kiln the colour of the pots could be controlled. The top of the kiln is a temporary affair of clay and wood which can be smashed after firing.

below: Two means of decorating pottery. Left is a wheel-turned pot on to which the decoration was applied free hand. This technique was favoured by most British potters. Right is a Samian bowl and above it a mould similar to the one it was made from. Clay was placed inside the mould in order to take the shape of the bowl and decoration. After removal extra clay was added to form the rim. The pot was then fired. This technique was favoured on the Continent.

Life in the countryside

Although the towns show most clearly the influence of the Romans, the countryside too was changed. Most people still lived and worked on the land. Even the rich town-dwellers liked to have their country houses. These houses, such as the one shown here, are known as 'villas' and were introduced to Britain by the Romans.

A villa was not just a farm-house or country retreat: it may be described as the centre of a farming estate which often had attached to it little workshops for making iron tools, or wooden ones, or pottery.

Life in the countryside was peaceful, as a rule, after the rebellion, and many villas were lavishly decorated. The photograph on page 18 shows part of a mosaic from the palace-like villa at Fishbourne in Sussex. That mosaic was made abroad and imported into Britain. The one shown on the opposite page was made by local craftsmen. It does not tell a British story, however, but illustrates part of the story of Romulus and Remus – the twins who (according to legend) founded Rome.

Roman engineers drained large areas of the Fens and some huge estates, run by government officials, grew up there and in the rest of the southern part of Britain.

The Romans introduced new crops such as millet, rye, oats, carrots, flax, peas and celery, also vines, plums, mulberry and walnuts. These benefited Roman and Britons alike. Roman roads helped farmers to take their extra crops to market.

Once again, it was in the southern part of Britain that Roman influence in the countryside was greatest. The ordinary farmer lived much the same as before, but at least he was free from war and slave-raiding.

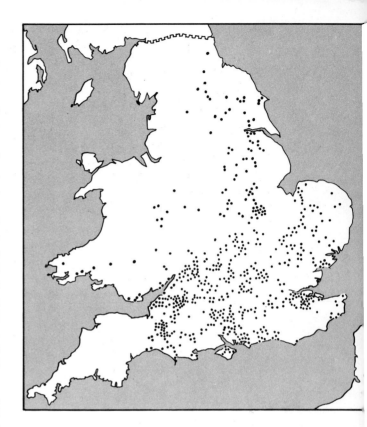

This map shows areas in which the villas were concentrated. A large group of rich villas is found around Bath, which was a favourite haunt of visitors from the Continent. No doubt many more villa sites lie still hidden under the ground.

This villa follows the typical plan with the main part of the building facing south and two wings built to trap the heat of the sun in a courtyard. There were usually two storeys, the lower one of stone and the upper one of wood. Some villas in Britain were the centres of sheep-rearing estates; others were nearer to being factories rather than farms. The majority of villas come between these extremes.

left: Roman farm implements found near Cambridge: a scythe (length 5 ft 4 in, 1·6 m), a plough coulter and reed cutters. The Romans also introduced the iron-tipped spade and the rake as well as an improved corn drying furnace.

Mosaic from Aldborough in Yorkshire. Stories from mythology were a favourite theme on Roman mosaics. Although it is likely that Britons made this one from pieces of natural stone and tile, mosaics were introduced to Britain by the Romans.

Two traditions come together

The Romans worshipped many gods and goddesses; and so did the Britons. The Romans usually let people worship whichever gods and goddesses they chose so long as they also sacrificed to the Spirit of the Emperor.

After a number of years the Romans and Britons began to combine the identities of their gods. For example, near Bewcastle, north of Hadrian's Wall, several altars to Apollo Maponus have been found. Apollo was the Roman god of light and music and Maponus was the local British god of music; so the two gods were worshipped as one.

Some favourite spirits were thought of as 'mother goddesses'. Local goddesses of, for example, the rivers were given Roman-style altars and worshipped by Britons and Romans alike. At Bath, the worship of the Roman goddess Minerva was combined with that of Sul, the local goddess of the springs.

Bronze head of Claudius possibly from a statue of the Emperor on horseback (height 12 in, 31 cm), date about AD 46. The eye sockets were probably inlaid with glass.

The bronze mask was found near the Brigantes' earthworks at Stanwick, Yorkshire. It was used as decoration on horse or chariot gear. First century AD, actual size.

right: The Bath Gorgon, from the pediment of the temple of Sulis Minerva; date about AD 200. The face and hair is native in style but there is also a large surrounding wreath in Roman style